Diving the Palos Verdes Peninsula

Phil Garner

Copyright © 2012 Phil Garner

ISBN-13: 978-1469981925

ISBN-10: 1469981920

The Palos Verdes Peninsula offers a wide variety of diving options. Between the sandy shore of Redondo Beach and the kelp forest of Cabrillo Beach lie rugged trails over rocky cliffs, moderate to easy exertions and trails that only a mountain goat or a psychotic diver would attempt. Many of these dive sites are available only by boat but for the intrepid backpacking diver, Palos Verdes has lots to offer. I have outlined many of my favorite local sites, but there are many more waiting to be discovered and enjoyed.

Table of Contents

1. Redondo Beach Artificial Reef
2. Veteran's Park
3. Palawan
4. R.A.T. Beach
5. Malaga Cove
6. Landing Craft
7. Crane
8. Haggerty's
9. Flat Rock
10. Avalon Wreck
11. Rocky Point
12. Honeymoon Cove
13. Christmas Tree Cove
14. Neptune Cove
15. Hawthorne Reef
16. Pt. Vicente
17. Marineland
18. Garden Spot
19. Abalone Cove
20. Archery Range
21. White Point
22. Radio Tower
23. Pt. Fermin
24. Cabrillo Beach
25. F. S. Loop

Driving down Pacific Coast Highway in Southern California, you will find many beautiful dive sites. Rocky shorelines and sandy beaches with kelp forests just offshore call to divers. As you head south past Malibu, the last available shore dive is Long Wharf at Will Rogers State Beach. The next shore dive is in Redondo Beach, where this book begins. The Palos Verdes Peninsula offers unique dive opportunities from deep canyons, artificial reefs, sloping sandy beaches, shipwrecks and sites where you might expect to see rock climbers rather than divers.

Artificial reefs in the Santa Monica Bay are mostly rock piles. In Hermosa Beach and Redondo Beach there are concrete pilings, dock floats, car bodies, concrete debris from freeway construction and two vessels. These reefs are home to life not found on the rock piles to the north.

Sandy beach entries are available from south of the Redondo Beach Pier to R.A.T. (Right After Torrance) Beach. Beginning at Malaga Cove, the shoreline becomes rocky and steep. Foot trails are the only access to shore from Haggerty's to Pt. Vicente.

Terranea Resort, at the former Marineland of the Pacific site has a long but easy walk to the shore, but you still need to contend with a rocky entry. The rewards can be incredible.

Abalone Cove and the Archery Range may be accessed via long paths. At White Point and Cabrillo Beach you can park close to the water. Cabrillo Beach has probably the easiest beach entry in California with restrooms and fresh water showers available.

Kelp forests near shore and man-made objects with metridium anemones and wolf eels just a few minutes away by boat make the Palos Verdes Peninsula one of the best places to dive in California.

Commercial dive boats from San Pedro and Long Beach take divers to Catalina Island each weekend with occasional trips to the outer islands. It was once rare to see a dive boat on the peninsula. In recent years a crop of smaller dive boats have begun to take advantage of all that Palos Verdes has to offer. Some of the larger boats have begun to join them. The Giant Stride, Westbound, Island Diver and Sea Bass now ply our local water. More divers have the chance to see the beauty of our local sites than ever before.

Westbound
westbounddiving.com/
13800 Bora Bora Way
Marina Del Rey, Ca. 90292
Toll Free (877) 699-0005
Local (310) 684-3871

Giant Stride
thegiantstride.com/
13900 Tahiti Way
Marina del Rey,
CA 90292
(310) 990-4702

Island Diver
rockypointfun.com/home.html
Rocky Point
310 Portofino Way
Redondo Beach, CA 90277
(310) 374-9858
(310) 376-4269 Fax

Great Escape
diveboat.com/
141 W. 22nd Street
San Pedro, California 90731
(866) 348-3262

Sea Bass
diveseabass.com/
Berth 75 Nagoya Way
San Pedro, CA 90731
(818) 652-5859

Area Dive Shops

Eco Dive Center
ecodivecenter.com/
4027 Sepulveda Blvd.
Los Angeles, CA 90230
(310) 398-5759
(888) SCUBALA

Pacific Wilderness
pacificwilderness.com/
1719 South Pacific Ave.
San Pedro, CA 90731
(310) 833-2422

Sea d Sea
seadsea.com/
1911 S Catalina Ave
Redondo Beach, CA 90277
(310) 373-6355

Dive N' Surf
divensurf.com/
504 North Broadway
Redondo Beach, Ca. 90277
(310) 372-8423
(800) 326-8423

New England Divers
nedscuba.net/index.htm
2936 Clark Avenue
Long Beach, California 90815
(562) 421-8939

Pacific Sporting Goods SCUBA Center
deepbluelongbeach.com/scuba/
11 39th Pl, Long Beach, CA 90803
(562) 434-1604

Sport Chalet
Long Beach Towne Center
7440 Carson St.
Long Beach, CA 90808
(562) 429-9560

Sport Chalet
Via Marina Marketplace
13455 Maxella Ave.
Marina Del Rey, CA 90292
(310) 821-9400

Sport Chalet
Village Del Amo
21305 Hawthorne Blvd. #205
Torrance, CA 90503
(310) 316-6634

Redondo Beach

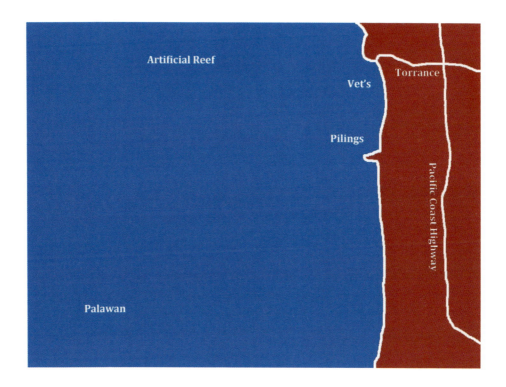

1. Redondo Beach Artificial Reef

In 1962, construction began on the Redondo Beach Artificial Reef. One thousand tons of quarry rock were dumped less than a mile off King Harbor. Over the years the reef was augmented with the addition of concrete pilings and dock floats, cement pipe and, in 1975, a retired Navy barge. The reefs are scattered over a wide area and are low enough to provide shelter to bottom dwellers but not high enough to attract game fish.

The concrete that rises a few feet off the sand is covered with club tipped anemones, *Corynactis californica* as well as scallops, hydroids, sponges and a few metridium anemones. Vermilion rockfish and lingcod cruise the edges of the reef and halibut may be seen in the sand.

The barge is home to gorgonian, which supports its own reef community. Simnia snails and skeleton shrimp feed on the gorgonian's polyps. Schools of senoritas feed on the shrimp. Nudibranchs can be found by looking under pieces of rusty metal flaking off the barge.

Small pebbles are scattered over the surface of the barge. You may wonder how they got there. Sea lions cavort on, in and around the barge, sometimes in large numbers. They seem to enjoy picking up pebbles from the sand and dropping them on other sea lions and unsuspecting divers.

Most of the artificial reef can be found in eighty feet, with the top of the barge at sixty.

Sea lions are a common sight on the barge.

Simnia snails, *Dalanovolva aequalis,* eat polyps and may be found laying multiple eggs on red gorgonians

The barge rests upside down. Holes have rusted through, allowing access inside. Lobsters and sea lions can sometimes be found inside, but not much else.

Concrete and rebar take on a psychedelic look when marine life takes over.

Metridium farcimen, commonly found on deeper wrecks, can be found on the Redondo Beach Artificial Reef.

Alpheopsis equidactylus

Car bodies become lobster habitat. This dashboard and fender make a perfect home for crustaceans. Visibility can be better near the barge due to the pebbly bottom.

Sea lion checks out divers on the barge.

Fried egg jelly, *Phacellophora camtschatica*.

Hermissenda crassicornis laying eggs on a red gorgonian.

Male and female sheephead, *Semicossyphus pulcher*

Blue rockfish, *Sebastes mystinus* swim in and out of the barge. Blue rockfish were once seldom seen south of the Channel Islands but are slowly making a comeback.

Barge

N33° 50.300   W118° 24.627

Pilings and rock piles

N33°50.210   W118°24.610

N33°50.286   W118°24.598

N33°50.230   W118°24.568

N33°50.294   W118°24.637

N33°50.258   W118°24.589

2. Veteran's Park

Vet's is the most popular shore dive in Palos Verdes. Divers can be seen each weekend and many weeknights hauling gear up and down the steps to the sandy beach. Many classes are taught here due to the shallow water near shore and relatively easy entries/exits. When the surf is up, exits can be deceiving. Waves create sandy "steps" near the water's edge. Even the most experienced divers get tripped up and find themselves crawling out of the water. Fortunately there are fresh water showers available at the restrooms located at the base of the stairs.

The edge of Redondo Canyon is very close to shore. Most divers begin their dives by surface swimming to the end of the nearby Redondo Pier and dropping into thirty feet of water, then making their way west toward the canyon. At sixty feet the sand drops off quickly, then slowly angles its way down to deep water.

Market squid rise from the canyon some winters and create one of the most exciting times for divers and marine life. Squid mate and attach their egg sacs to the muddy bottom, usually between fifty and one hundred feet deep. Octopus, sheep crabs, bat rays, sea lions, small fish and the occasional blue shark gorge themselves on the dead and dying squid. The relatively bare sand comes alive with feeding frenzy.

Squid boats drop their nets just outside King Harbor at night. Divers should keep clear of the boats, which are easily seen with their bright lights. When sea lions are present, the crews of the squid boats will drop seal bombs, small explosives to scare the sea lions. It doesn't seem to have much effect, although the noise and concussive charge rattles divers pretty well.

North of the main stairs in forty-five feet is an area known as the Salad Bowl. Kelp, trash and other detritus is swept here and becomes home to a myriad of life. Red octopus, sarcastic fringeheads, crabs, shrimp and a variety of nudibranchs can be found. Vet's is one of the few places where divers will leave trash during an underwater cleanup. Bottles, traffic cones, cinder blocks and other items dumped here become home to many of the animals at Vet's.

At the south end of the beach, just before you reach the jetty are pilings from the old Redondo Beach Wharf #3. The pier was dismantled in June, 1926 when lumber companies moved their operations to San Pedro. Today, only five pilings remain, but they are an oasis of life in the sandbox of Redondo Beach. Some rise several feet off the bottom. Crabs, small fish and a variety of shrimp make their homes in the pilings. Corynactis anemones and barnacles feed on the passing current. The pilings are difficult to find, but if you enter between Topaz and Sapphire Streets the pilings may be found between thirty-five and forty-five feet. If you find one the next one will be in an east-west direction. Divers sometimes tie lines between the pilings, making them easier to find.

Metered parking is available along the embankment of the beach and in the main lot located at the Esplanade just west of Pearl Street and Catalina Avenue. Restrooms are closed at night, but the icy cold showers are available any time.

Juvenile giant sea bass, *Stereolepis gigas,* are sometimes found just beyond the surf at Vet's

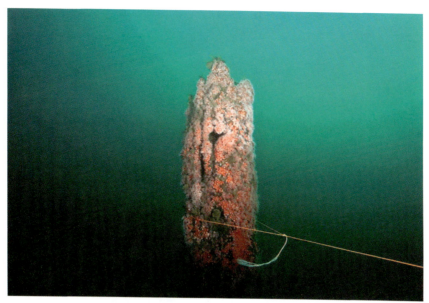

Redondo Beach Wharf #3 piling

Sarcastic fringehead, *Neoclinus blanchardi,* peers out from his home

Market squid and egg sacs

Market squid egg sacs

Two-spot octopus, Octopus bimaculoides, makes its home in a traffic cone

Acanthodoris rhodoceras

Polycera hedgpethi

Janolus barbarensis

3. Palawan

The Palawan was one of over six hundred Liberty ships constructed during World War II. They were designed to carry material and supplies to our troops and allies. Most are long gone, but one, the Lane Victory can still be seen docked in San Pedro.

The Palawan was stripped down to her 441 foot hull before being sunk as an artificial reef off the coast of Redondo Beach in 1977. Holes were cut in the bulkheads and top of the ballast holds to allow divers access to each compartment. The outer hull is covered in colorful corynactis anemones. Small shrimp and crabs can be found among the anemones. The top of the bow has red and golden gorgonian growing sparsely. Small rockfish and sculpin rest beneath their branches. Much of the surface and interior is covered by silt. Care must be taken when penetrating the ship to avoid clouding the site.

For such a large ship on the edge of Redondo Canyon there are remarkably few large fish. For many years the fishing barge Isle of Redondo was anchored over the ship. Monofilament line can be found throughout the wreck.

In 1978 rubble and concrete pilings were added to the reef. Lobster and halibut can be found between the pilings.

The Palawan sits in 125 feet at N33° 49.181   W118° 24.977

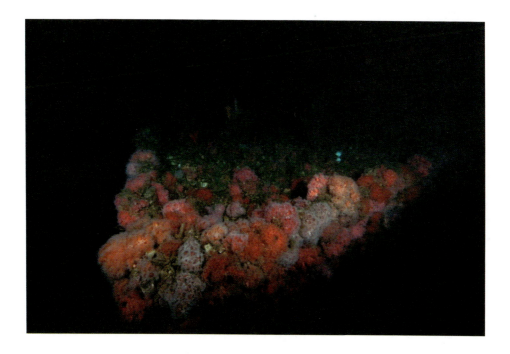

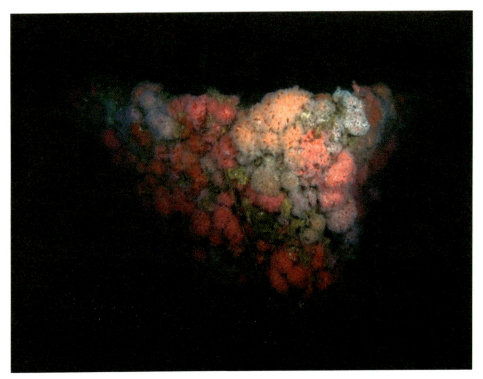

Corynactis californica covers the outer hull on the bow.

Looking for photo subjects near the gorgonians.

Outer hull with interior ribs

Vermilion rockfish, *Sebastes miniatus*

West Side

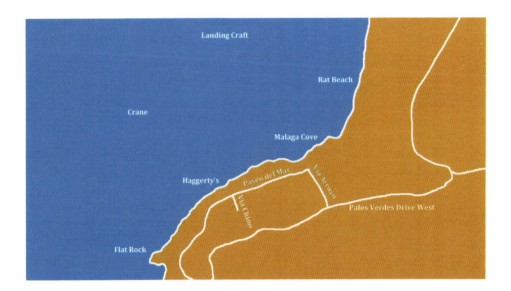

4. RAT Beach

Right After Torrance Beach is the last sandy beach available to the public before reaching Cabrillo Beach. There is a small shallow reef just beyond the surf zone between the white rocks on the hillside just north of the trail from Malaga Cove and the parking lot at Via Riviera and Paseo de La Playa. Enter from the sand four hundred feet south of the parking lot and the reef begins a few hundred feet from shore. This is a shallow site with the deepest parts of the reef found in forty-five feet. When the surf is down and surge is at a minimum you can spend nearly two hours on a single tank here. The white rocks on the hillside are actually compressed diatoms from an age when the ocean level was much higher. Looking at samples through a microscope will reveal fascinating silica exoskeletons of prehistoric algae.

Lifeguard tower at the south end of RAT Beach

Diatomaceous earth, Diatomite

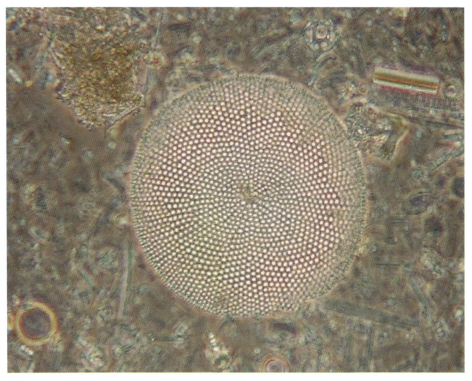

Diatoms

Malaga Cove

During the late summer and early fall, when the peninsula is getting hit by south swells, many divers head to Malaga Cove. One of only two north facing beaches in Southern California, Malaga Cove is a popular site for those wishing to dive the kelp forests of Palos Verdes without hiking down a goat trail.

Malaga Cove is where the rocky shoreline of the Palos Verdes Peninsula actually begins. The west facing sandy beaches of the south bay give way to rocky reefs and thick kelp of the peninsula. The reef at Malaga Cove is a series of long ridges running parallel to shore, separated by sand channels. Bat rays, halibut, torpedo rays, angel sharks and guitar fish are sometimes encountered in the sand here. The reefs also aid in navigation, as you can follow one out to deeper water and return on the other side or an adjacent ridge.

The rocks support a thriving kelp community of fish, octopus, lobster, snails and crabs. The reefs here are the only natural reef on the peninsula where I have seen a moray eel, although some divers have found one near Marineland.

Visibility is sometimes poor at Malaga Cove, especially after rain. A small creek empties into the ocean at the base of the cliff. Better visibility can be found in the outer edges of the kelp in twenty-five feet. You can judge visibility from the gazebo atop the cliff before descending the trail. On days with great conditions you can see the layout of the reefs and even spot nearby R.A.T. Beach reef.

Entry over the slippery rocks should only be made during high tide. The bottom remains shallow for quite a distance from shore, making it difficult to remain upright. Many divers choose to enter and exit from the sandy beach north of the site. It makes for a longer swim to the kelp, but helps to avoid injuries.

Parking is available in the Malaga Cove School lot at 300 Paseo del Mar. Other than a port-o-potty near the baseball fields there are no facilities.

After assessing conditions from the gazebo, hike down the steep paved road to the north. If conditions warrant you may enter from the rocks or continue on the dirt path to the sandy beach. The hike may seem long, but compared to most trails on the Peninsula, Malaga Cove is a walk in the park.

Malaga Cove School

The gazebo offers a great view of the south bay

Trail head

Trail crosses over the small creek

Dirt trail leads to the sandy beach

Looking south from R.A.T. beach

Avoid diving near the creek

Kelp forest just offshore

Rough Piddocks, *Zirfaea pilsbryi*, are found at the edges of the reefs

Torpedo ray, *Torpedo californica*

Garibaldi, *Hypsypops rubicundus*, are found everywhere on the reef

6. Landing Craft   LCM3

Alvin Kidman was a local salvage operator who operated out of Los Angeles and King (Redondo Beach) Harbors. He was known to cut a few corners to make a profit, including skipping town while owing thousands of dollars in fines to both harbors. He would even tie his boats to docks owned by other boaters rather than pay for his own slip. He purchased obsolete Navy craft and converted them into salvage barges, floating Playboy-type cruisers and anything else that could make a quick buck. Once his vessels were no longer profitable he was known to dispose of them by sinking, and not always far from shore. Some of his vessels were left in the muddy bottoms of the harbors, hence the fines.

He purchased the S.S. Avalon which had been cut nearly to the waterline, added a crane to the aft deck and used it to salvage parts of the Dominator wreck. The Avalon sank during a storm on September 16, 1964. Another vessel he was reported to use on the Dominator was an LCM3 landing craft with a mobile crane onboard. Both the crane and landing craft now rest 2000 feet apart off the west side of Palos Verdes.

The landing craft now sits upright in sixty feet of water off Malaga Cove. Other salvagers, the kind with brass on their mantles at home, removed as much as they could. What remains has become a nesting site for the locals. Red octopuses guard their eggs under rusty plates. Male garibaldis charge anyone who approaches their nests, and nudibranchs lay ribbons of eggs next to their favorite food source. During the summer, giant sea bass frequent the small wreck. Look in the sand surrounding the wreck for torpedo rays. Animals rarely seen around Palos Verdes can be found here, including swimming file clams.

Many times my dive buddies and I have been photographing some small creature on the wreck, only to see a giant sea bass or sea lion checking us out. The landing craft can be found at N33° 48.562   W118° 24.331

File clam, *Lima pacifica*

Pacific Electric Ray, *Torpedo californica*

Octopus rubescens with eggs

Octopus eggs

Gorgonian covers the open gate

7. Crane

Moray eels are common at Catalina Island and Laguna Beach, but are rarely found around Palos Verdes. The crane off Haggerty's is one of the few places where you can find them. I saw two eels fighting in mid water here once. I kept my distance from their undulating bodies and sharp fangs. One eel can be found in the extrusion at the highest point on the wreck. The other is usually hidden inside the crane base. The crane is home to lobsters a few months out of the year, but divers should use caution when reaching inside the rusting hulk. Morays have been known to leave bad scars.

Garibaldis build their nests on the tires still attached to the crane. When their eggs are present, look closely for tiny orange dots with eyes. Hermit crabs gather in small groups on the crane and surrounding rocks. If you look at one of the rocks closely you will find snails, nudibranchs and tiny amphipods grazing. If you look too long, several sheephead will show up to see what you've discovered. There is also a giant sea bass that makes an occasional appearance here.

The rocks near the crane are small and cannot support kelp during periods of swells or surge. At times, the crane may be surrounded by thick kelp, but it all but disappears with the first storm of the year.

At a depth of fifty-five feet, scuba divers will have ample time to explore the nooks and crannies of the crane. It's not a large wreck, but there is plenty to find if you look closely.

N33° 48.301   W118° 24.534

Moray eel, *Gymnothorax mordax*

Kelp rockfish take shelter under the corynactis-covered tires.

Red Rock Shrimp, *Lysmata californica*

Spiny lobster, *Panulirus interruptus*

8. Haggerty's

J.J. Haggerty, owner of the lavish Haggerty's Department stores of Los Angeles, Beverly Hills and Pasadena built this Italian style villa at 415 Paseo Del Mar in 1927 as a summer home. His upscale stores featured grand staircases and large chandeliers. The Great Depression took a heavy toll on Haggerty and he was forced to sell his mansion. By the 1950s it was purchased for $60,000 by the Neighborhood Church. Their congregation had grown too large for their previous place of worship at Malaga Cove School.

Behind the church is one of the largest kelp beds on the peninsula. Visibility can be a bit better here than at Malaga Cove to the north. The bottom is a relatively flat boulder field with its deepest depth at only thirty-five feet.

Sheepcrabs are plentiful at Haggerty's. Some are very large and seemingly brazen. They will walk right toward a diver as if to play chicken. They usually win.

Opaleye are numerous in the shallow water near shore, with calico bass and garibaldis dominating the kelp. Side gilled slug *Berthella californica* can be found in great numbers on the outer reef.

Other than diving from a boat, there are two ways to access Haggerty's. Both are difficult. There is a trail one block west of the church near the corner of Paseo del Mar and Via Chino. In some spots a polypro line, inner tube or whatever is currently used to aid surfers and divers during their climb is needed. The other option is to enter from the rocks near the bottom of the swim club at Malaga Cove. Both require walking over strewn beach stones to reach the water. Exits usually require crawling out after falling on the wet rocks.

Several years ago a wooden staircase was built between Malaga Cove School and Haggerty's. I used it and appreciated it…a lot! Unfortunately someone thought it was a great place to spray paint graffiti. The stairs were removed after only a few weeks.

Haggerty's on a flat day. Surfers often call "Hag's" their own during winter storms.

The upper section of the trail is the easy part

Line used to aid the climb. Easiest entry is directly in front of the cement block.

Berthella californica

Male sheep crab, *Loxorhynchus grandis,* carrying its mate

9. Flat Rock

Flat Rock owns the distinction of having one of the toughest accesses in Palos Verdes. The trail is steep, and in places no more than a few inches wide. Once you reach the rocks you have to choose between scrambling over the rocks to enter from the beach where any wave will trip you up or leaping into the water from the point. It is possible to make a giant stride entry from the point, but it must be timed well to avoid being swept back into the rock. Night dives add the problems of losing your footing on the trail and having your tires slashed for parking too close to someone's "turf". Six cars were vandalized during one of my last night dives here.

Parking is located along the 600 block of Paseo del Mar. The upper section of the trail is level and wide. Don't be fooled by this. The bad news comes soon enough. The small foot path drops off quickly toward the rocky point below. Move slowly and carefully down this trail. The nearest hospital is miles away.

You can judge conditions before making the hike by watching the waves hitting the shore in the cove. This is where you will be making your exit. It is a shallow, slippery exit over algae covered rocks hidden under the surf grass. Why would anyone want to dive here? The answers lay under the surface.

If you want it bad enough to go through all that, the rewards can be satisfying. Flat Rock offers near shore diving unlike most of the peninsula. The reefs are tall, some as much as ten feet off the sand. Lobsters, harbor seals, bat rays and even a reported large gray fish with a triangular dorsal fin have been spotted.

On calm days the kelp forest rivals the best you will find in Southern California. Sunlight creeps through the amber canopy, lighting up the reef as if it were on a stage. Schools of blacksmith hover overhead while calico bass and sheephead follow divers' movements.

Upper section of the trail. Note the symmetry of the point leading out to Bit Rock. Parallel reefs are common to the west side of Palos Verdes. Look for bat rays in the wide sand channels between the reefs. Depths to forty-five feet outside the kelp.

This is where the fun begins. Free divers seem to enjoy diving Flat Rock a bit more than scuba divers do. Lobster hunters won't mind as long as they come home with a bag of bugs.

Tongva-Gabrieliño Native Americans lived in Palos Verdes for over eight thousand years. They made canoes for fishing and traveling to the offshore islands to trade goods. Artifacts can still be found on occasion. I found a grinding bowl made from a stone that was likely found on the beach. It was buried in the sand in forty feet of water, indicating it may have fallen from a canoe

Artifacts from more recent civilizations can also be found here.

Polycera atra

Calico bass, *Paralabrax clathratus*

Rocky reefs perpendicular to shore are common on the west side.

Rubberlip Seaperch, *Rhacochilus toxotes*

A large variety of invertebrates are found throughout the peninsula. Flat Rock has a large proportion of them.

Club tipped anemones, *Corynactis californica*

Kelp rockfish, *Sebastes atrovirens*

Rocky Point

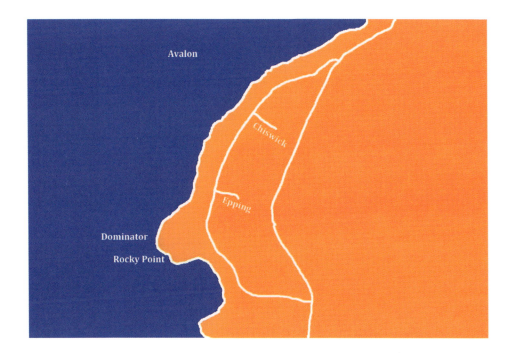

10. Avalon Wreck

Sitting on the rocky bottom in seventy feet lays the wreck of the S.S. Avalon. Built in 1891 she was first launched as the S.S. Virginia. The Virginia carried passengers between Chicago and Milwaukee for twenty-seven years before being requisitioned by the Navy in 1918. Renamed the U.S.S. Blueridge, the ship was not used until being sold to William Wrigley in 1920. Now called the S.S. Avalon, the passenger ship became a fixture in Southern California. The Avalon, along with her sister ship the S.S. Catalina, ferried passengers between Wilmington and Catalina Island before being retired in 1951.

The Avalon was sold for scrap in January of 1960. Most of the superstructure and machinery was removed. A fire gutted most of what remained on July 18, 1960, partially sinking the ship in her mooring. Alvin Kidman purchased the hull and added a crane to salvage the Dominator. On September 16, 1964 the Avalon broke anchor and sank for a final time a half mile off Chiswick Road.

What remains on the bottom bears little resemblance to the grand ship that once carried thousands of passengers to Catalina Island. The bow rests on its starboard side while the crane is the only recognizable portion of the stern. Ribs and scattered plates separate the two sections. Lingcod have found the plates to be a nice place to live. It is not unusual to see more than a dozen lingcod on one dive. Schools of Rubberlip seaperch, *Rhacochilus toxotes,* are found around the crane year round.

Piddocks, gorgonians, snails and a few nudibranchs can be found on the bow. Photographers will find much more macro subjects on the rocks inshore from the wreck.

Avalon bow   N°33 47.313   W118° 25.682

Stern   N33° 47.360   W118° 25.685

Avalon bow. Visibility is often poor on this wreck, but can be excellent at times.

Inside the remains of the bow

Crane and gear wheels at the stern

Gorgonians add color to the rusty hull

Rubberlip seaperch are common near the crane

11. Rocky Point

Rocky Point is popular with free divers for two reasons. Spearfishing can be good and shore access is nearly impossible with scuba gear. There are two trails, neither of which leads directly to the point. North of the point is the trail at Epping Road. This will take you a few hundred yards north of the point. It's a long walk over rocks and rusty debris from the Dominator wreck. It is an interesting hike to check out the bow and some of the heavy equipment left over from the salvage operation.

The other option is to hike down the surfer trail at Lunada Bay. If you try this, let the local surfers know you are diving. They don't take kindly to non-locals surfing the cove. If the surf is up at all, try another dive site. Diving at Rocky Point is shallow until you get to the middle of the huge kelp bed where the bottom gradually drops to thirty feet. If conditions are good you can check out the stern section of the Dominator. It peeks out of the water at low tides.

The reef extends far offshore, so watching for boat traffic is a must. Jumbled boulders, mini walls and sand make up the bottom, while a thick kelp canopy covers most of the area. There are times when you cannot get to the Dominator because the kelp is too thick to crawl over.

White seabass come into the area during the spring, with Yellowtail following them in the summer. When these fish are in, so are the divers. It is common to see dozens of free divers each day at Rocky Point. In spite of the thick kelp, a float and flag is highly recommended. Game fish also bring in lots of boats.

Scuba divers will enjoy the extended bottom time in the shallow water. This gives you plenty of time to explore this massive reef system. Because this reef sits on a point, currents can be strong. Currents and high tide can bring in some amazingly clear water. Looking down the kelp from the surface will remind you of Catalina. Blue water, amber kelp and schools of blacksmith welcome divers. Look for octopus, lobsters and an occasional abalone under the rocks.

Steep trail near Epping Road

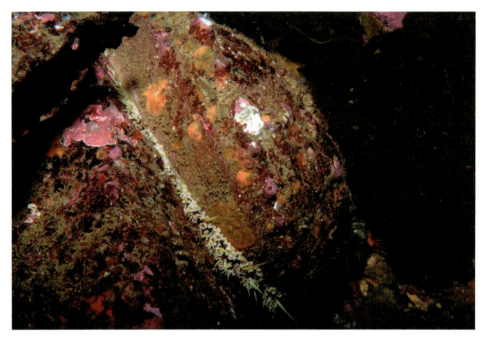

Abalone can be found on the rocks.

Kelp crab hides within the kelp fronds

Southwest Side

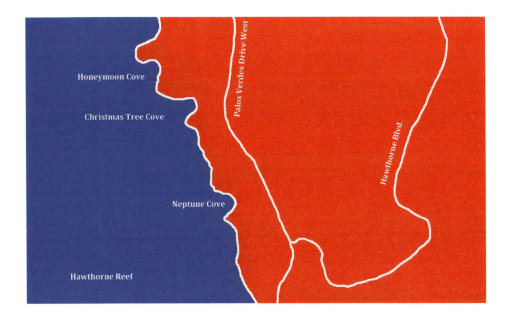

12. Honeymoon Cove

The reefs at Honeymoon Cove are similar to those at Christmas Tree Cove and Lunada Bay. The trail is shorter but much steeper. The upper section requires handholds and sometimes sliding feet first a few feet.

Leopard sharks and bat rays can be seen in the shallow reefs. The best diving requires a long swim to the kelp off the northwest point. The reef extends for hundreds of yards offshore, offering a variety of habitat.

Boat traffic can be heavy outside the cove. It is best to avoid surfacing away from shore.

Upper section is difficult to traverse

13. Christmas Tree Cove

If you are looking for better visibility than most shore diving sites and do not mind a little effort, Christmas Tree Cove is just the place. Once known as Patterson's Cove after a local resident, the name Christmas Tree became more commonplace. There was a triangular shaped pine on the hillside at one time. A few years ago, a landslide took half of the road and a large section of the cliff and dropped it onto the beach below. The trail on the west side was unaffected. It is still as difficult as it always was.

Visibility can be assessed from the trailhead before making your descent. If you can't see the submerged rocks clearly from the top of the cliff it will not be worth the effort to dive. The rocky bottom near shore offers excellent snorkeling opportunities. I have spent hours free diving along the shore between Christmas Tree and Honeymoon Cove. Leopard sharks, bat rays, opaleye and garibaldi are often seen in the shallows.

Christmas Tree Cove facing east toward Pt. Vicente

Park on Paseo del Mar near the intersection with Via Neve. The trail begins at the edge of the cliff. There are a couple of spots where you may need to use your hands, but most of the trail is easily negotiated, albeit steep and long. Even when snorkeling with only mask and fins, the trail seem to take forever to climb. Take your time entering the water. The entry is made up of slippery rocks.

Divers enter over the rocky shoreline

There are some fish and urchins to look at as you snorkel out to the first reef in the center of the cove. This reef is a large rocky area that is always covered by a thick kelp canopy. Large rocks are home to nudibranchs, sponges, fish and kelp. Soupfin sharks sometimes gather in this area. Visibility here averages a few feet more than most sites around Palos Verdes.

The best diving at Christmas Tree Cove requires a longer swim. Offshore from the east side of the cove is the edge of an expansive reef system. The northern edge of the reef breaks the surface at low tide. Beyond this high spot are overhangs, some resembling caverns large enough to allow divers to crawl into. Lobsters frequently are seen far inside these caverns. This section of the reef continues south. The east side of the reef has several vertical walls as tall as ten feet. It is fun to swim over the edge and get the feeling of flying weightless. There is a sand channel separating this section from the larger reef to the west. This western reef extends beyond the point at Honeymoon Cove.

Save enough air for the swim back toward the beach. You don't want to exert yourself too much before making the strenuous hike back up. There are no facilities nearby, so bring drinking water and a gallon or two of rinse water. You will be hot and your gear will be muddy by the time you return to your vehicle.

Christmas Tree Cove high spot   N33° 45.606   W118° 25.341

The cost of diving here

The long and winding road

Blue rockfish, *Sebastes mystinus*

Cuthona divae

Chestnut cowrie, *Cypraea spadicea*

Rough Patch shrimp, *Pandalus stenolepis*

14. Neptune Cove

Neptune Cove is not for the faint of heart. The trail is one of the toughest in Palos Verdes. Entry over rocks and tide pools can be treacherous and the swim to the best diving is a long haul, but I know divers who have done it. Parking is east of the trailhead, and access to the water involves ignoring the signs and climbing over or through the steel fence.

The trail leads to a large tide pool. Entry can be made here or from the cove to the east.

Neptune Cove has a series of large boulders and mini walls just offshore from the tide pools. Nudibranchs, kelp, sponges and gorgonian blanket the reefs. Giant Sea Bass and Torpedo Rays occasionally cruise through the kelp.

The most interesting feature here is the underwater arch, located at the southwest end of the reef near the east side of the cove in fifty feet. The arch is big enough to drive a car through. Its wide ceiling is a good place to spot uncommon nudibranchs such as *Dendrodoris behrensi*.

Spanish Shawl, *Flabellina iodinea*

Blacksmith, *Chromis punctipinnis*

Top of the arch

Inside the arch

Visibility can be quite nice at Neptune Cove, but even moderate swells can reduce visibility to near zero. It is best to dive here on only the calmest days. The parking lot is located at 27 Calle Entradero, Rancho Palos Verdes. Boat diving is the easiest way to dive Neptune Cove. The arch is located at N33° 45.076 W118° 25.070

15. Hawthorne Reef

If Walt Disney designed a reef for Southern California, he would have filled it with every colorful creature found in the area. Every inch of the reef would be covered with corynactis anemones, creating a quilt of green, red, orange and pink, and leaving just enough room for barnacles, nudibranchs, gorgonians, sponges, worms, hydroids and more fish than a Seattle market. If he had been successful, his reef would look a lot like Hawthorne Reef.

Listed in fishing charts as Barber Pole, Hawthorne Reef sits a third of a mile offshore between Neptune Cove and Pt. Vicente. The barber shop used as a line up is long gone from the Golden Cove shopping center at the end of Hawthorne Blvd. Ross Overstreet coined the name while making dive maps. The reef is almost directly in line with the southern end of Hawthorne Blvd. It was not long before most dive boat captains began calling the reef by the new moniker.

Hawthorne Reef is a jumbled pile of rock resembling a craggy island in the middle of a sandy ocean. The rocks jut skyward in places, resembling giant thumbs hitching a ride. Some top out at fifty-five feet, some twenty-five feet off the sand. Many rocks have tunnels and cavern-like cutouts. There are some holes large enough for a diver to swim through.

When visibility is good, the reef comes into view from twenty feet below the surface. As you approach the reef you may have a hard time deciding where to go first. Schools of blacksmith flitter above the rocks, while garibaldi and small rockfish dash through the holes. Lingcod, scorpionfish and cabezon may be found resting on nearly every rocky outcropping. Colorful treefish hide in the small holes, occasionally peeking out at the divers.

Nudibranchs, blue ring top snails and hermit crabs add even more color to the overload of hue. Photographers often make two dives to shoot macro and wide angle here.

There are also a lot of manmade items to be found at Hawthorne Reef. One section of the reef has remnants of a seine net, including several large brass rings. Coke bottles have been found here as old as eighty years. The reef has been popular with fishermen as well as divers for many decades.

Due to its offshore location, current can be a problem here. If the down line becomes taut seconds after hitting the bottom it is probably a good day to try Buchanan's Reef instead. When conditions are good, Hawthorne Reef is one of the best sites to dive in Southern California. You won't find this much color at recreational diving depths anywhere else on the peninsula.

N33° 44.814   W118° 25.234

Blacksmiths surround the reef

Female sheephead blending in to the colorful background

Mating pair of *Mexichromis porterae* nudibranchs

A dive light will bring out the rich color of the reef, even on daytime dives

Gorgonians fill in the lower sections of the walls

Red beard sponges, *Microciona prolifera*, add bright textures to discover

Anemones feed on plankton in the passing current at Hawthorne Reef

Southside

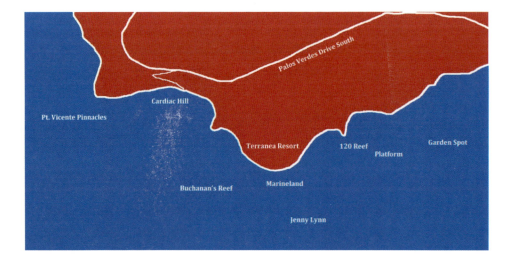

16. Pt. Vicente

Once a popular fishing spot, Pt. Vicente became part of a Marine Protected Area on January 1, 2012. No living creature may be taken. It is now easier to dive here without having to watch for the dozen fishing boats overhead.

Whale Rock breaks the surface just offshore from the point below the lighthouse. The rocky reef extends west and southwest from here, with dramatic pinnacles to explore. Some of these pinnacles rise from depths of sixty to eighty feet, reaching within ten feet of the surface. Deep water is found close to the southern end of the reef and occasionally pelagic animals will be found here. I have seen two thresher sharks on the reef and gray whales surfacing between the pinnacles and shoreline.

Many of the pinnacles are isolated from the reef. You can explore a vertical wall of one rock and spot others across the sand. Invertebrates carpet the rocks. Blue ring top snails are plentiful, and macro photographers will fill their cards with colorful nudibranchs found throughout the reef. Blacksmith, calico bass and small rockfish are found year round. Kelp grows from the shallow section of the reef. You can look down the kelp to judge the conditions before diving.

Strong currents can be a problem, so it is best to dive Pt. Vicente during slack tide. I've made a few dives here when we aborted after resembling flags on the downline, having to pull our way down hand over hand. When the water is calm, Pt. Vicente Pinnacles can be dramatic.

N33° 44.328   W118° 24.895

Until becoming part of the Pt. Vicente Marine Protected Area the next cove was known as Pt. Vicente Fishing Access. Most divers know it as Cardiac Hill. The trail is straight, graded and has a few wooden steps and a rail to hold, but that doesn't make it a stroll. It is long and steep, and when you finally reach the shore you still have a long walk over rocks to get to the entry points. The good news is that the diving on either side of the cove can be quite nice.

In the center of the cove is a small reef with a few fish and some kelp. If the hike has worn you out you may elect to dive here, but you will be missing out on the reason divers make this trek. The west side of the cove has a nice rocky reef three quarters of the way to Whale Rock. The reef extends down to sixty feet at the southern end. Invertebrates, rockfish and kelp forest inhabitants are found in plentiful numbers. I know of one diver who has made it all the way out to the reefs beyond Whale Rock. That is certainly an endurance test, especially in scuba gear.

The west side of the cove has some beautiful pinnacles just offshore. One large rock rises forty feet out of the water, creating spectacular white water explosions as the waves crash into its base. It the sea is calm, the pinnacles may be reached just offshore from this rock. The reef drops down to forty feet here, with a few smaller reefs to the southwest in sixty feet. If you continue east into the next cove you will reach Buchanan's Reef. Marine life found at Cardiac Hill is much the same as most sites on the south side of Palos Verdes. Sea stars, rockfish, kelp, sponges and nudibranchs are numerous.

There are restrooms located at the trailhead, with plenty of parking spaces. After diving, you may visit any of the local restaurants at Golden Cove Center or Terranea Resort. Go to the Pt. Vicente Interpretive Center to learn about the local geology, history and marine life. The American Cetacean Society takes a whale census on the rear deck of the center.

San Diego dorid, *Diaulula sandiegensis*

East end of the cove with Terranea Resort on the hill above

Bottom of the trail facing east

Lower section of the trail

East side with Catalina Island in the background

West side with Pt. Vicente and Whale Rock in the distance

17. Marineland

The best diving at Marineland can only be reached by boat, or a long swim to and from the Point. Buchanan's Reef extends from the west side of the property out to eighty feet of water. The rocky reef reaches thirty feet off the bottom in places. Kelp, anemones, rockfish and nudibranchs blanket the entire reef. Buchanan's is also a great spot to find anchors. The rocky bottom has a long history of capturing ground tackle from the myriad of fishing boats that used to frequent the site. When diving Buchanan's it is always a good idea to move your anchor to a sandy area at the beginning of your dive.

N33° 44.015   W118° 24.155

Marineland of the Pacific opened to the general public on August 27th, 1954. Over the next thirty-three years it provided fun and education for millions. After years of financial hardship and several ownership changes, Harcourt, Brace, and Jovanovic, owners of Sea World purchased the property and promised to keep the park open. They closed it on February 11, 1987, six weeks after the sale was complete, moving most of the animals to their park in San Diego. Because it was no longer legal to capture Orcas in the wild, Sea World needed to find its performing killer whales elsewhere. Orky and Corky, the stars of Marineland were renamed Shamu and Namu.

The lot at Long Point sat deserted for the next two decades. Only the Catalina Room, the former Marineland Restaurant remained open for weddings and banquets until 2004. I began diving shortly after Marineland closed. On most days I had the only car in the parking lot. In 1990 more divers appeared thanks to an article in the California Diving News. Marineland soon became one of the more popular dive sites of Los Angeles County.

Diving Marineland is not a walk in the park. Entry and exit can be challenging, if not hazardous. The cobbles in the cove shift with every storm, making a once easy entry difficult. Even on calm days, the wet rocks and surge will knock down the most surefooted diver. If you haven't crawled out of the water onto rocks while waves slam you down and pull you back in, you haven't dived here enough. Many divers have suffered broken bones here, even in benign conditions. Exiting requires baby steps. Wait for a lull in the water movement and then take small steps toward the shore. Once out of the water, keep moving to higher ground.

Some days are not diveable. Three feet of surf is not bad at many sites, but can be hazardous at Marineland. Even if you were to make it out, surge and low visibility would make a bad dive even more dangerous. When the sea is calm, Marineland offers some of the best diving in Southern California.

In June 2009 Terranea Resort opened on the former Marineland site. Although the diving can still be spectacular as well as challenging, amenities on the shore are much improved. A public parking lot leads to graded trails down to the water. Restrooms, snack bar and a fresh water shower are located midway to the cove.

From the cove, the closest reef is known as the Garden. It was once an urchin barren but thanks to divers removing the urchins it is now a thriving kelp forest. Depths range from zero to thirty-five feet, making the Garden an ideal shallow dive or a great swim-through on your way back from the Point.

Garibaldis, calico bass and other typical reef fish are found here. Look closely in holes and cracks for shrimp, octopus and small blennies. Anemones, gorgonian, sponges and Christmas tree worms cover most rocks here. Schooling fish frequent the edge of the kelp, while bat rays and angel sharks can be found in the sand nearby.

I found a tiny pink abalone on a rock here. After feeding it a kelp frond on most dives it grew to over eight inches. Until recently it was on the same rock for more than ten years.

As of January 1, 2012 the entire coastline of Marineland out to three miles is a Marine Protected Area. It will soon be as pristine as it was when Marineland first opened.

East of the cove is a reef commonly referred to as the 120 Reef due to its location from the beach. It extends offshore to about forty-five feet. The 120 Reef is home to kelp, sponges, feather duster worms and many sunflower stars. Many divers choose to dive this reef due to its proximity to shore. It is only a ten minute surface swim here compared to the twenty-five minute swim to the Point.

The sandy plains surrounding Marineland can be interesting to explore. Jellies, giant sea bass, torpedo rays and mantis shrimp share the sandbox with sea pens, globe crabs and snails. It's a worthwhile diversion to check out the sand away from the reefs.

Mantis shrimp, *Hemisquilla ensigera*

Diving at the Point is what makes Marineland an incredible dive site. Boulders and pinnacles are home to a variety of invertebrates, but the Point is best known for its nudibranchs. I have found seventeen species on one dive here.

Flabellina trilineata

The best diving is at the south end of the reef in sixty to seventy feet. You can enter from the Point or make the one quarter mile swim from the cove. On calm days divers prefer the shorter swim. In the shallow water near the cement piling at the Point lie the remains of the Newbern. It ground into the shallow rocks near shore on October 14, 1893. Only a few pieces of rusty iron remain near the piling, with some chain and anchor in thirty feet off the southeast corner of the Terranea Hotel.

Because Marineland lies on a point, currents can be common here. Diving at slack tide is recommended, but great conditions can be found at any time. There is deep water offshore, so the constant upwelling keeps the water several degrees colder than sites with little relief such as Laguna Beach. It is not uncommon to have a ten degree difference on the same day. Visibility ranges from near zero during moderate surf to well over thirty feet on the best days.

Long Point   N33° 44.073   W118° 23.890

Cove facing east

Restrooms, snack bar and shower

Steps and rocky shoreline of the cove

The Garden, 120 Reef and Platform locations

Monterey dorid, *Archidoris montereyensis*

Blue-banded Goby, *Lythrypnus dalli*

Vermilion rockfish, *Sebastes miniatus*

Honeycomb rockfish, *Sebastes umbrosus*

Treefish, *Sebastes serriceps*

Black-eyed goby, *Coryphopterus nicholsi*

Polyclad worm, *Pseudoceros luteus*

Dendrodoris behrensi

Christmas tree worm

Rainbow nudibranch, *Dendronotus iris*

Sea Hare, *Aplysia californica*

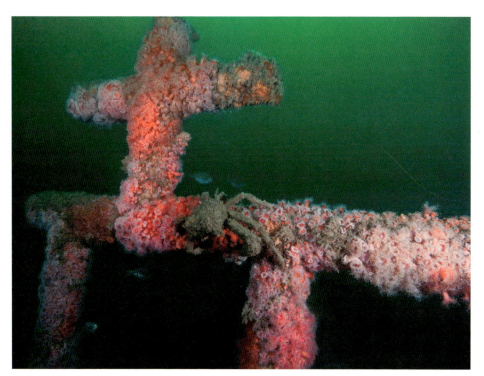

Offshore from the 120 Reef is the Marineland Platform. The platform was a floating steel dock that was originally dumped in fifty feet of water south of the cove. It was first discovered by divers Jim McCabe and Christian Lopez on February 6, 2005 while searching for the 120 Reef. They were told there was a reef in forty-five feet outside the cove, but didn't have the heading. When I asked them for the location they each had different ideas of where it was. I narrowed it down to a few square acres and made several searches before locating it. After tying cave line from the platform to the Garden it became a new site for beach divers to enjoy.

The steel structure is home to corynactis anemones, nudibranchs, crabs and scorpionfish. The wooden deck was rotted but still provided surface for a small kelp forest and a rest stop for a large halibut.

I had to replace the line a few times, and then one day the platform itself was missing. Gary Fabian, who had located the UB88 in 2003, used the same sidescan technology to find the platform. It had been snagged by a squid boat, and then dragged 800 yards eastward. It now sat in over eighty feet off the 120 Reef, minus the wooden deck. A few years later it was once again snagged and moved by another squid boat. This time it was spun around and now sits at eighty feet from its last resting place. Nets covered the entire structure, trapping squid and any bird or fish that swam into it. We cut the net to allow the squid to escape, then notified Kurt Lieber, founder of the Ocean Defenders Alliance. He and his volunteers removed most of the net, making it safe for divers and marine life again. Merry Passage and I placed a buoy on the site to discourage fishermen from dropping nets here and to help divers locate it.   N33° 44.150   W118° 23.438

Merry Passage places float over the platform

Cuthona divae

Polycera tricolor

18. Garden Spot

Between Marineland and Abalone Cove are luxury homes with spectacular views. The hillside below the homes is a sculptured landscape. A lush garden, complete with walkways and benches has been constructed on the steep terrain. Just offshore from this garden is a long, thin reef. Averaging less than twenty feet wide, Garden Spot reef stretches more than one hundred feet perpendicular to shore. The reef is littered with abandoned lobster traps and the associated lines. This debris is now home to an assortment of small creatures. Nudibranchs, hydroids, bryozoan and algae cover the metal wires of the traps.

Tube anemones surround the reef in sixty-five feet of water. Sand bass and crabs patrol the sand while calico bass and sheephead cruise the top of the reef. Look in undercuts and cracks around the outer edge of the reef for nudibranchs.

N33° 44.236   W118° 23.167

Zooanthids move in and take over gorgonians

Serpula columbiana

Black eyed goby, *Coryphopterus nicholsi*, with *Triopha catalinae* nudibranch

Phoronopsis californica

Mating pair of *Mexichromis porterae*

Octocoral, *Alcyonium rudyi*,

Tube anemone, *Pachycerianthus fimbriatus*

Portuguese Bend

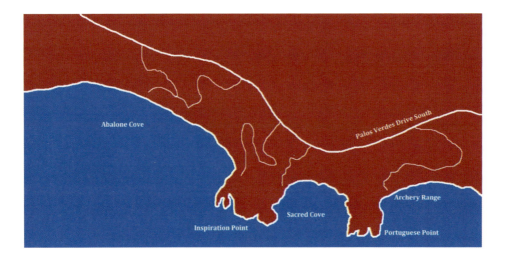

19. Abalone Cove

This is a nice spot to get in a dive while spending the day exploring Portuguese Bend. The diving at Abalone Cove is shallow and there is not as much to see as other nearby sites unless you make a longer trek across the rocky beach and dive near Portuguese Point. The reef directly in front of the Lifeguard stand is a short swim after an easy entry. There is not much relief, usually only a foot or two, but kelp grows here and supports a fledgling marine habitat. Calico bass and small sheephead cruise over the low reef. Tunicates, sponges and worms dominate the reef.

Most of the cove is made up of a sandy bottom where you may find halibut, crabs and an occasional torpedo ray. Diving near the point is more rugged, but any surf at all will make this nearly impossible due to surge. You may also make a longer surface swim and explore the kelp forest of the west side of Abalone Cove.

To reach Abalone Cove, park in the lot at 5970 Palos Verdes Drive South and follow the trail down to the water. After diving you may wish to explore the area. There are trails leading to the tops of Portuguese and Inspiration Points where you can enjoy spectacular views of Catalina Island and maybe spot whales. Another trail leads down to Sacred Cove where you can explore the tide pools and sea caves. At low tide you can see through the cave to the other side of the point.

Across Palos Verdes Drive South is Wayfarer's Chapel. Lloyd Wright, son of Frank Lloyd Wright designed this church to allow worshipers to view the trees surrounding the chapel. He was inspired by the view from a diner's skylight in the Redwood Forest.

Hedgehog hydroid, *Hydractinia milleri*

Giant Acorn barnacle, *Balanus nubilus*

20. Archery Range

The South Bay Archery Range is one of those fun, off the beaten path dives. There is no public parking nearby, it is a long hike to the water, visibility is rarely more than a few feet and the only facility on site is a port-o-potty. It remains one of my favorite beach dives in Palos Verdes because of the ruggedness of the site and the surprisingly large number of marine animals found here.

Entry is easy, as the small cove is protected from most swells. Within ten yards of shore you can find Hopkin's Rose nudibranchs grazing on the rocks in shallow water. Follow the reef that parallels the cliff to the point and you will encounter calico bass and large sheephead that seem to know they are safe due to the low visibility.

If the sea is calm you can enter the caves at the tip of Inspiration Point, but even moderate surge can push you into the rocks. Lobsters crawl over the rocks outside the cave at night. Be careful where you place your hands, as many large horn sharks can be found resting on the bottom.

A car shuttle is required to dive the Archery Range. Drop off your gear with your dive buddy at the locked gate and park at the Abalone Cove upper lot one mile west. There are three options to access the cove. A graded dirt road leading from the gate winds its way down past the targets and port-o-potty. If you haul your gear in a wagon or on a dolly, this is the way to go. There is a trailhead near the ski jump, the section of Palos Verdes Drive South that makes a short, steep climb west of the gate. Between the gate and trail is a drainage pipe that you can also hike next to. Carrying gear in a cart or on your back, plus air temperature during the summer will help you decide which option is best.

Hopkin's Rose, *Okenia rosacea*

Berthella californica

Black-and-Yellow Rockfish, *Sebastes chrysomelas*

A whaling station once operated at the shore just east of the Archery Range

The former whaling station is now a private beach owned by the Portuguese Bend Club

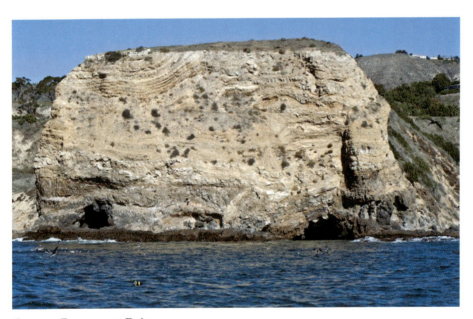

Caves at Portuguese Point

San Pedro

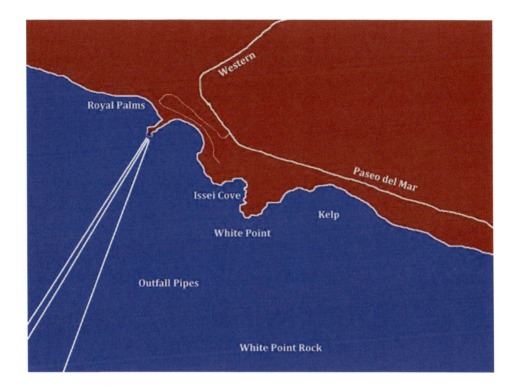

21. White Point

One of only two dive sites on the peninsula that do not require climbing stairs or a trail, White Point has a different look than any other site. Sulfur bacteria filaments attach to the substrate near hydrothermal vents near the outer edge of the cove and on the reefs just offshore. These filaments are similar to other vacuolate (fluid-filled cells) bacteria found near deep water vents. The White Point filaments are unique in that they do not store internal nitrate.

For information about the sulfur bacteria, go to
http://aem.asm.org/content/70/12/7487.full

Sulfur bacteria

Entrance to the lower parking lot. Early arrival allows for use of cheaper, metered parking near the water. Once the guard arrives the price increases.

White Point/Royal Palms County Beach is located at 1799 Paseo del Mar, San Pedro.

Brothers Tojuro and Tamiji Tagami, along with land owner Ramon Sepulveda began construction of the White Point Hot Springs Hotel resort and spa in 1917. Visitors bathed in the sulfur hot springs and swam in the enclosed salt water pool. Boats would transport fishermen from the pier to an offshore barge beyond the kelp. During the 1920s, the resort was one of the more popular destinations in Los Angeles County.

The Great Depression, severe storms and the 1933 Long Beach Earthquake led to the demise of the resort. During World War II the Japanese immigrants at White Point were taken to internment camps. Remnants of the pool can still be seen in the tide pools and the fountain that once adorned the hotel now rests in the upper parking lot.

White Point offers several areas to dive. Directly off the old pool are shallow, parallel reefs where lobsters hide in the overhangs and kelp. Surge can get extremely strong here, so scuba divers tend to leave this area to the free divers.

Remains of the shipwreck Melrose are scattered offshore in front of the Lifeguard tower. Surf, low visibility and entry from the point make this a difficult dive.

Most divers elect to dive from the east cove. Shallow rocks make walking difficult, therefore it is common to see divers pull themselves along on their stomach until reaching deep enough water to fin. At high tide you can use the flat concrete blocks at the shoreline to enter or exit.

Not much marine life can be found inside the cove. Urchins, octopus and Opaleye make up most of the population. When you reach the white bacterial filaments you are near the mouth of the cove. Black sand and sulfur vents are found along the edge of the reefs. On days when there is a strong sulfur scent in the air you can feel a temperature difference at the vents. There is a low-lying reef to the south, but the best diving is to the east.

Mini walls line the outside of the cove, with large overhangs and kelp to the east. Further to the east the reefs flatten out and the kelp gets thicker. Giant Sunstars, sand rose anemones and schools of fish are found in this area. Large Smoothhound sharks and guitarfish can be found on the sand.

A landslide in 2011 wiped out the fire road leading to the east side of the point. The road was the best access for night dives at White Point, as the main gate closes at dusk. I had one of my favorite night dives here. During one of the rare times when visibility was great my buddy Jeff Shaw and I encountered a giant sea bass, which came up to my face three times.

Restrooms are located at the western end of the park, near the Lifeguard tower. Fire pits and picnic areas are also available.

The best shore diving is in the kelp east of the cove.

Concrete blocks in the foreground make entries easier

Restrooms and picnic area at Royal Palms

Sponge covered scallop

Norris' top snail, *Norrisia norrisi*

Two spot octopus, *Octopus bimaculoides*

Tiny abalone shell on a bat star

Painted greenling, *Oxylebius pictus*

Another interesting offshore dive is the outfall pipes leading from near the Lifeguard tower. Four concrete pipes lead to deep water. The pipes are embedded in quarry rock and are home to gorgonian, rockfish and nudibranchs. The pipes can be found on Google Maps.

Gorgonian and kelp on the outfall pipe

Blue ring top snail, *Calliostoma annulatum*

Clown dorid, *Triopha catalinae*

Offshore from White Point is a rock that resembles a miniature Hawthorne Reef. Roughly the size of a city bus, White Point Rock is a nursery for nudibranchs and rockfish. Juvenile fish swim right up to you as if to ask what you are doing there. Several nudibranch species are found here including a large population of Ategema alba, uncommon in most sites around the peninsula. Much of the rock rises a few feet vertically from the sand, with a section on the southwest side ten feet tall. On top of the rock is a flat area where a couple of Rubberlip sea perch make their home. Gorgonian and red beard sponges add another foot of relief to the reef. Although most fish here are juveniles, it hasn't stopped fishermen from dropping nets.

Smaller rocks are nearby, some covered with fishing nets. I removed a large net on one of my first dives at White Point Rock.

Depths reach seventy feet, with the high spot around fifty-five feet.

N33°42.468 W118°19.098

Volunteers haul up a large net abandoned from White Point Rock

Ategema alba laying eggs

Gopher rockfish, *Sebastes carnatus*

Green water of White Point Rock

Sand Rose anemone

Starry rockfish, *Sebastes constellatus*

Menacing looking lingcod rests on the rocky bottom

Serpulid worms add beauty to even the loveliest reefs

Black eyed goby rests on a rock scallop

Pt. Fermin

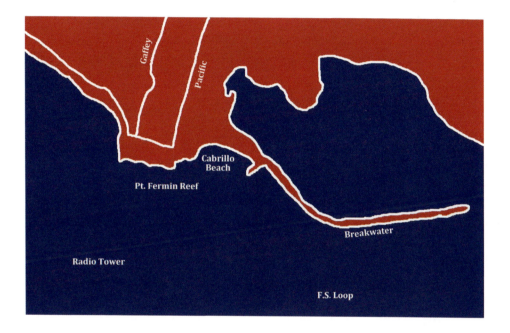

22. Radio Tower

The Radio Tower is one of many items that were disposed of in the deep water off Pt. Fermin. Fortunately for divers, it was not dumped beyond recreational diving depths. It is too short to really be called a radio tower. It was likely a RADAR tower. The top of the structure is horizontal; perhaps a support for a dome or a water tank. The tower lies horizontally in just over one hundred feet with the highest point in sixty feet. Corynactis and metridium anemones cover every inch of the structure. Crabs and nudibranchs crawl between the anemones, grazing for tiny bits of food.

Because the tower sits very near the point, currents can occur here. It is recommended that you time your dive for slack tide.

N33° 41.608   W118° 17.678

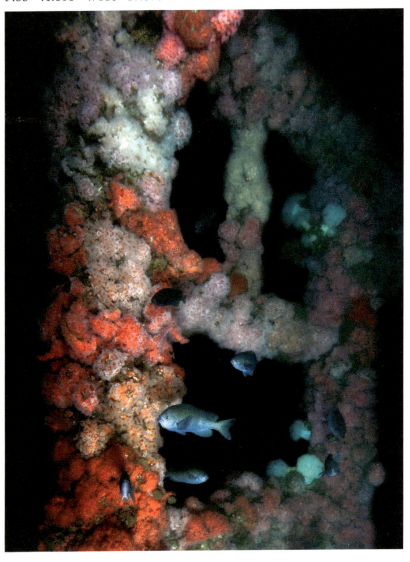

Anemones, scallops and nudibranchs are in abundance on the tower.

Pt. Fermin Reef

The reef off Pt. Fermin is shallow, but far from boring. A large plateau in twenty-five feet drops away five feet along the edges. These cracks and mini walls are home to lobsters. Although most of them are short, a few keepers can be found. I once came to the surface with three lobsters in my bag, which was amazing, considering I only caught two. One had molted inside the bag. I returned the soft-shell crustacean to a hole where it could remain until his new exoskeleton hardened.

Finger sponges and tunicates can be found on nearly every rock near shore. Offshore the reef gradually drops to over fifty feet, where boisterous sea lions from the nearby buoy are quick to harass divers.

The shallow kelp bed is a popular fishing spot with private boaters, so a float and dive flag are recommended.

Free diving access is available from the trail west of the light keeper's house on the south side of the point, or from Sunken City to the east. It's a long and dangerous haul with scuba gear. Pt. Fermin is known to experience accidental falls or suicide jumps every year. The cliff face is vertical in many places, so any unnecessary weight would cause an imbalance in your future.

N33° 41.936 W118° 17.501

Pt. Fermin Lighthouse

4. Cabrillo Beach

Although visibility is usually limited at Cabrillo Beach it can be a nice experience for those wishing to make an easy dive. Waves are rarely more than a foot high and the packed mud bottom makes walking in and out of the water as easy as you will find anywhere. The rocky reef and kelp forest begin less than fifty feet from shore and extend well beyond the distance most divers will swim. Piddocks, urchins, anemones, snails and a few nudibranchs are found on the rocky substrate. Schooling fish and harbor seals flash past in the limited visibility. Remains of a shipwreck lay in the outer edge of the thick kelp forest. A small jetty on the east side of the beach makes an easy night dive. Lobsters and octopus crawl out of their lairs at night as the rocky embankment comes alive.

A long surface swim is required, but you can also shore dive the Los Angeles Breakwater from the east end of the beach. Most animals and plants found in Palos Verdes can be seen in concentrated areas along the breakwater.

Topside attractions at Cabrillo Beach will interest even non-divers. Wind surfing in the afternoons, pier fishing and tide pool walks are available at the shore. Cabrillo Marine Museum is a treat to check out. Many aquariums and exhibits show off the local marine life, and a touch tank is available for the entire family.

The boat launch is located at the north end of the parking lot. During spring and summer months, nudibranchs can be found in great numbers mating and laying eggs on the kelp fronds at the surface next to the dock.

Barbecues and fire pits are located throughout the park.

Cabrillo Beach is located at 3720 Stephen M. White Drive in San Pedro.

Breakwater access with fishing pier

Bath house and Lifeguard station on the beach

Outdoor showers are at the edge of the sand and grass.

Jetty at the east end of the beach

Harbor seal

Piddocks

Nudibranch hunting at the boat launch

Melibe leonina mating and egg-laying on kelp

25. F.S. Loop

The F.S. Loop was a wooden lumber schooner built in 1907. For three decades it hauled lumber along the west coast until it was damaged in a storm in 1936. It was refitted with a gasoline engine and worked the next three years in Mexico as a seal processor. After returning to Los Angeles, the Loop sat in the harbor until it sank in 1946. It was raised, then towed and sunk off the Los Angeles Breakwater.

The Army Corps of Engineers require sixty feet of depth clearance for harbor approaches. The Loop, resting upright in seventy-feet required explosives to lever her. What remains is scattered wreckage with a few large sections. It doesn't sound like an exciting dive, but the Loop has become an oasis on a silt seabed. Nudibranchs, sponges, gorgonians and anemones blanket the exposed portions of wreck. Silt covers much of the lower wreckage. Schools of fish can be seen hovering over the site when visibility is good.

Good visibility is not common here, unfortunately. With the silt bottom, sweeping currents from Pt. Fermin and outflow from the harbor during low tide the site is usually bathed in silt. On occasions of good conditions, the old wreck gives divers a look at her surprising amount of life.

N33° 41.832   W118° 15.977

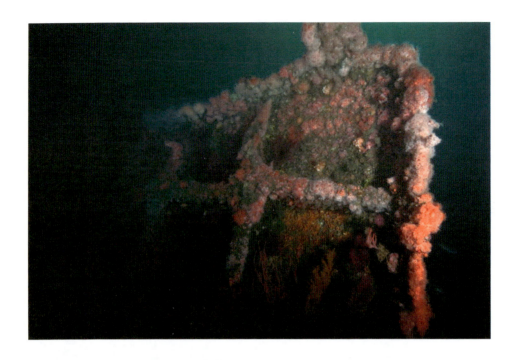

Nudibranchs such as the *Doriopsilla spaldingi* and *Tritonia festiva* are found in abundance on the F.S. Loop.

Bibliography

Cardone, Bonnie and Smith, Patrick Shipwrecks of Southern California Menasha Ridge Press 1989

maureenmegowan.com

California Department of Fish and Game

Portuguese Bend Beach Club

California Wreck Divers

Kalanetra, Karen M., Huston, Sherry L. and Nelson, Douglas C.
Novel, Attached, Sulfur-Oxidizing Bacteria at Shallow Hydrothermal Vents Possess Vacuoles Not Involved in Respiratory Nitrate Accumulation

Made in the USA
Charleston, SC
11 May 2012